Change Your Mind
Change Your Destiny

The eight habits of success that will help you create better relationships, more health, more wealth, and more happiness.

Dr. Jay LaGuardia

FIRST EDITION

http://www.drjaylaguardia.com
http://www.jaylaguardia.com

ISBN-10: 0692607218
ISBN-13: 978-0692607213
(Think More, Be More Inc.)

DEDICATION

To my wife Pam, and my children: Alyse, Anthony, and Taylor, for their constant support and love. You have always inspired me to become a better husband and father. You are my core, my passion. I love you guys. I am also thankful to all those who have encouraged me to write this book and share this message.

CONTENTS

ACKNOWLEDGMENTS

Special thanks to W.J. Vincent II for your mentorship and encouragement. Your advice, technical support, and excitement for this book pushed me to overcome every obstacle. I am thankful for all your help and, more importantly, for your friendship.

PREFACE

This book was written with the intent to dispel the myth that personal growth is hard. It doesn't have to be, it just takes know-how, commitment, and dedication. Personal growth and change are never easy but, with the appropriate tools, anybody can achieve them. If a guy like me, who grew up with challenging circumstances, with all the built-in excuses that most of us have, could willfully change my destiny by applying the eight habits taught in this book, anyone can.

Your past is your past, and that's where it needs to remain. The windshield in your vehicle is twice as large as the rear window for a reason—because we should spend most of our time looking forward. It is the part of our lives that we have control over and that we are able to affect based on a new vision we might have for ourselves. We get to choose every day how we show up, either as a victim or victor. I believe with these eight habits, the odds of creating the life of our dreams have never been greater. How do I know this? Because I've lived it, I've taught it, and thousands of others have also experienced these life-changing results. Many of these concepts have been around for years, but I've been able to devise a simple way of understanding them and, more importantly, applying them to life.

So, who should read this book? Well, everyone of course! If you have picked up this book, it's because you have a curiosity and a desire to grow. If you have ever struggled with poor or low self-esteem, a lack of confidence, or an inability to define your life's purpose, then this book is for you. If you've ever experienced past challenges (and who hasn't), then this book is for you. If you've ever struggled financially or had trouble with relationships, this book is for you. If you've ever had big dreams, or a lack of dreams, this book is for you. What I'm really saying is that everyone can benefit mentally, physically, spiritually, and financially from the eight habits discussed in this book.

Please join me on this journey of personal growth and self-fulfillment. You'll be glad you did.

CHAPTER ONE
"AN INTRODUCTION"

"You may be disappointed if you fail,
but you are doomed if you don't try."

~ BEVERLY SILLS

The eight habits of success that will help you create better relationships, more health, more wealth, and more happiness has been in the making for quite some time. To be more specific, for about 50 years, which is how old I am at the time of writing this book. This book is a story of the transformation of an individual through life's journeys and experiences. While somewhat remarkable, it's certainly not unique to me. However, it's a story which I'm hopeful can inspire others to know that they can achieve anything they desire with the proper tools and a little help here and there.

Obstacles in life occur all the time, but it's how we handle them that determines our destiny. We can allow those obstacles to define us, or we can use them as springboards to learn and grow and move beyond; even reinventing a new and better version of ourselves. When we're experiencing the challenges of life, it's often difficult to see beyond them as we get consumed by everything going on around us. Often our view becomes clouded, and our thinking so jaded, we cannot see through the process. This whole book is about setting up and providing the tools necessary to learn what it takes to get over life's challenges. Is it easy? No. After all, life isn't easy. There are very few places in life that arm you with the tools necessary to learn how to become personally successful.

Schools certainly don't teach you these tools. Most parents would love to if they were familiar with these habits; unfortunately, they can only share what they know. Society doesn't teach them. In fact, in many ways, our culture mocks personal growth and self-help programs as a sign of weakness. However, the opposite is true.

I've been studying personal growth, self-improvement, and the habits of success for more than 30 years. During this time, I've been able to apply these tools and habits in my life, as well as mentor and coach others in these simple steps. What I've observed is that those who apply the lessons within this book are able to achieve any dream they have, or any goal they set. The formula is not new, nor is it unique to this specific book. However, I learned as a person who, prior to beginning my own journey of personal growth, was totally clueless on what to do and where to begin, let alone what resources could help me. I believe that you'll find everything within this book you need to begin your journey so that you can create the life of your dreams.

In my own life's journey, I've faced many difficulties. The eight habits in this book were powerful tools that not only saw me through those dark times, but made me stronger. I will share with you in Chapter Three how important mentors are in providing a foundation to get you started. Mentors can manifest in many forms; they can be a coach, teacher, spouse, or friend. It could be a tape or even this book. (Well, considering that it's the 21st century, maybe not a tape — perhaps an MP3 or podcast.) Fortunately, although technology may change, the value of mentors doesn't!

Potential mentors exist all around us. These are people who are willing to share their experiences with you. You'll be amazed how many there already are and who can't wait to help you on your journey.

Mentors are a great resource who will help you understand how they made their dreams and goals come true while helping you better define your own. In Chapter Two, you'll see that dreams are the fuel that ignite the passion to take action. Dreams spark new ideas in which you create something better for yourself, your family, or humanity.

Dreams are the fuel for future achievement. They keep you motivated in the present and inspired for the future. Have you stopped dreaming? I find that people who are stuck in life have stopped dreaming. Dreams are nothing more than images of your soul's desire. As life occurs, it's easy to get disconnected from our dreams. In Chapter Two, I will show you how to dream again. Our dreams are inspired by our highest values. In Chapter Six, you'll learn how important defining your values are for setting goals. Values are the engine behind every decision we make. This book can provide you with the skillset necessary to identify and prioritize your values.

Once you've defined your values, the process in Chapter Nine, goal-setting, becomes far simpler than you've ever experienced it before. Many of us know that goal-setting is an important part of success, but few of us actually do it, and even fewer write them down. When you have a defined set of values, your goals are easier to establish.

Chapter Seven covers meditation—the tool that changed my life more than any other. Most people are not aware of how powerful meditation can be, and even fewer still actually practice it. Meditation was the driving force behind my transformation from being anger-driven in life, to discovering an inner calm and peace. This provided the impetus for understanding who I was and why I'd always reacted so angrily to life's experiences.

Chapter Eight discusses the importance of affirmations. The human brain is constantly engaged in dialogue. Unfortunately, the vast majority of that dialogue is rooted in negativity. In Chapter Eight, you're going to learn how to change that internal dialogue from negative to positive using the simple and effective strategy of affirmations.

A shift in consciousness begins with an attitude of gratitude. This is covered in great detail within Chapter Five. I believe gratitude is the single strongest virtue that can begin to change a negative consciousness to a positive one. Chapter Eight will show you how gratitude can unlock all things that are good in your life, and how that same gratitude can attract the right people, places, and things to make your every dream and goal become a reality.

In Chapter Four, it's all about your authentic self. Most of us live our lives to please others. Many of us find ourselves trying to live up to others' expectations of what our life should be according to them. Even if they mean well, this rarely results in being true to our authentic self. Unlocking our authentic self is a revealing and joyous experience. There is nothing more fulfilling than getting to know self, and even better is to live true to self. Chapter Four will help you find that authentic self — the true essence of who you are that exists deep inside you.

At the conclusion of each chapter you will find a series of steps that will get you started on implementing each habit into your life. In addition to the actions steps, I provide you four questions that help you examine previously held beliefs you have about each of the eight habits. Take some time and complete these questions before you move on to the next chapter to get the best results. Unless we understand why we think the way we do, we have little chance of creating change.

Most books written about personal growth lack real tools that you can apply immediately. I really want the time you've invested reading this book to have the greatest impact possible for your life. This book is not a passive experience but one which, if applied as designed, can change anything about yourself you desire.

I'm excited and humbled that you've chosen this book to be a part of your life's journey. My ultimate goal with this book is to share these eight steps that anyone can apply to their life and overcome any obstacles or challenges that may be holding them back. Each chapter will provide simple action steps that you can apply immediately to begin your transformation. Remember: personal transformation doesn't happen overnight; it's a lifelong evolution. Hopefully, you'll have "Aha!" moments when reading this book. Perhaps a thought or idea will present a new image of who you want to become. If this book inspires you to create better relationships, to improve your financial status, or clarify your life's purpose—anything that leads to finding your true happiness—then the purpose of this book has been fulfilled.

CHAPTER TWO
"DREAMING"

*"To dream by night is to escape your life,
to dream by day is to make it happen."*

~ STEPHEN RICHARDS

It was a warm summer afternoon and the ballpark was full. I emerged from the dugout to the roar of the crowd and stepped to the plate with the game on the line. The bases were loaded with two outs in the bottom of the ninth; it was the ultimate chance to be a hero. The pitcher was staring me down as I prepared for my moment of destiny. I dug into the batter's box, readying myself for that moment of destiny. The pitcher entered into his windup and delivered the pitch; with a mighty swing came a thunderous whack as I hit the ball as hard as I could. The ball soared into the blue sky above; the left fielder hopelessly raced to the fence and could only watch as the ball sailed into the stands. The entire crowd went wild; I was the hero of the moment, hitting the game-winning grand slam. As I approached home plate, my team was jumping up and down, basking in this incredible moment of triumph. It was a magical moment. I was 10 years old. Upon the crack of my bat, we had become district champions. Even though, like many of you, I've had recurring dreams since childhood of becoming a professional athlete, that experience at a mere 10 years of age was arguably the closest I would ever experience to living that dream.

My entire life, I'd dreamed of becoming a professional baseball player, and that grand slam moment seemed to cement the possibility of it becoming a reality. Unfortunately, my skill level did not meet my passion for the game and, even though this dream never became a reality for me, it helped to instill dreaming on a regular basis within my life. This habit would serve me well in many different ways throughout the years to come.

So, let's take a moment together and reflect back to a time as a child when you had your own dreams and aspirations. Do you remember how you felt? If you're like me, you felt energized, enthusiastic, and even invincible—like you could accomplish anything. It didn't matter how far-reaching or crazy your dream was, it was still your dream, and no one could take it away from you.

Getting back to reality for a minute, Dr. Sigmund Freud, the legendary founder of psychoanalysis, theorized that dreams are driven by an unconscious desire for wish fulfillment. Along those same lines, I personally believe dreams are the images and desires of the subconscious mind, waiting to be fulfilled. They sometimes require us to be courageous enough to take big and bold action if they are to become our new reality.

There is no such thing as a silly or frivolous dream, and putting energy into them should never be considered a waste of time. Having dreams are necessary to see beyond our current reality. They provide us an opportunity to get lost in our imagination, and to develop the portion of our brain that allows us to think boldly and outside the realm of possibilities. If for some reason you don't think this is possible, just consider some of history's greatest pioneers.

Let's start by thanking God for people who are willing to dream big, like Michelangelo, who saw "The David" in a block of marble, as opposed to everyone else who just saw a piece of rock. Or consider all the amazing innovators like Henry Ford. He is singlehandedly responsible for the creation of the assembly line, which systematically resulted in lower costs, eventually allowing every American to own a vehicle, and launching the industrial revolution. Then there is my personal favorite, Leonardo da Vinci, the original Renaissance man best known for his painting of *The Last Supper*. He was also a philosopher, an engineer, and an inventor. Many of his inventions we have perfected and still use today, such as the helicopter, the tank, and solar-powered energy. When did he ever sleep? For those of you who need a more recent example, consider Jeff Bezos, the founder and CEO of Amazon.com who has revolutionized e-commerce. (This is one of my wife's personal favorites due to the convenience of online shopping!)

What do all of these amazing people have in common? They were dreamers. They were willing to challenge themselves and think big and differently, even in the face of criticism and ridicule. They had the courage to step forward and pursue their dreams, even against great odds.

Maybe you don't have the desire to change the world. Maybe your goal is to go to college or improve your relationship with your spouse or children. You see, it doesn't really matter what it is. These fundamentals of change and personal improvement remain the same, nonetheless. Excellence is not a genetic predisposition. Many of these great innovators were self-made. Some might not have been born any special talent, skill, or ability. In fact, to start with, with the only difference between them and most of us was their self-belief and willingness to pursue their dreams. What further differentiates them from most is their persistence and commitment to stay the course. Let's all remember that excellence is a mindset, and dreaming is a skillset and a habit, just like the other eight habits you'll be reading about in this book.

Dreaming must be learned and then put to practical use. Even though most people think dreaming is something we do only at night, we can learn to dream often. We move in and out of dream states more frequently than we know. Think about it. How often do you catch yourself daydreaming in the middle of a conversation? Many times you may become completely detached from everything in your environment, including the conversation itself. Then you find yourself brought back into your current reality by those around you who have noticed you've taken a momentary mental vacation. There's nothing wrong with this. This is good, it's healthy, and it's normal and should actually be encouraged. Okay, perhaps not driving down the interstate at 80 miles per hour, but it should be supported within a safe and controlled environment. You see, we don't have to be asleep to dream.

When we take these momentary mental vacations, we're moving into alpha brain waves. This is explained in greater detail during Chapter Seven, "Meditation," but here is a brief explanation of two of the brain cycles called alpha and beta. Beta brain cycle is when you're present and conscious in your current environment, or, in other words, a normal awakened state. The next phase, alpha, is when you step beyond and move into a conscious dreamlike state. It's not hard to access alpha brain waves. Often, it's very simple to do so by taking a couple of deep breaths in, exhaling them slowly, and refocusing your mind. This allows you to slow your thoughts down. The alpha state redirects our thoughts to someplace different, imaginary, and creative. This heightened creative state is from where new ideas originate. It's where thoughts pop into our head and new intentions are created.

Children do this easily because they don't put any limitations on their thoughts and easily embrace the concept of dreaming. Unfortunately, in today's world, this type of behavior is often discouraged or worse yet, some of the most imaginative children are being classified as attention deficit disordered. So, what is in fact a part of a child's normal brain development, and which is also a major foundation for future success, is many times being classified as a disease. Here's a scary thought for you—if Einstein were born today, he would most likely have been heavily medicated. Mozart might have found himself institutionalized. Many of the most influential figures throughout history may have never been able to reach their full potential if they'd been born today. Be sure not to confuse creativity in dreaming with a deficit disorder. Think about it. As a kid, who doesn't fantasize about being a professional athlete, princess, superhero, actor, or even a rock star? Detaching ourselves from reality to something new and different is a very important step in the development of the brain. The more we do it, the more that portion of the brain develops. Therefore, the more times we engage the creativity of our mind, the easier it becomes. Those who develop this skill tend to be the greatest innovators and the biggest visionaries.

The funny thing is, as you watch children participate in this behavior, they free themselves of judgment and ridicule for their dreams and fantasies. They couldn't care less what anyone thinks. They're so caught up in expressing themselves that they have no time for judgment, whether it's their own or someone else's. As adults, we need to embrace and encourage this, not only for children, but for ourselves as well. More importantly, think about the last time you really dreamed, leaving your current reality behind, and thought about something crazy or different. It's not very common for adults. Why is that? Our minds get cluttered and filled with everyday activities. All the mundane habits and behaviors of trying to survive in our daily lives leave no room for creativity and dreaming. We get so caught up in the activities of being an adult, such as work, school, paying bills, raising a family, and taking care of a home, that we dream less and less. Dreaming is too important of a success habit to allow this to happen.

We need to set time aside each day to clear our minds, and slow our thoughts, so we can tap into the creative portion of the mind. This will allow us to dream more, while thinking bigger and bolder. Dreaming is an essential ingredient to eventually living our destiny. In fact, I would argue that it is impossible to fully live our destiny without experiencing and practicing the process of dreaming. Dreaming unlocks our soul's desire to be fully expressed in our lifetime. Dreaming helps give meaning to life. Dreaming creates excitement, and the possibility of creating something new. There is no better process of connecting to your purpose.

When I work with clients, I ask them, "What is your purpose?" They usually shrug their shoulders, or give me that deer-in-the-headlights look. They're so busy being busy they've taken very little time to contemplate this question. Sadly, the most common response is that they don't know. Worse yet, they don't know how to connect to their purpose, or even how to begin to understand it. The next logical question I ask is, "Do you dream regularly?" As one might have expected, those who are disconnected from their purpose, or have altogether never identified it, don't dream. Those who have dreamt previously, unfortunately, don't remember their dreams or have stopped dreaming altogether a long time ago. So, I explain that dreaming is not something you do only at night. In fact it is important to understand if you really want to connect and fully understand your purpose in life, you must learn how to actively dream again. While working together, I teach my clients the skill sets they need to do this, which allow them to find or reconnect with their life's purpose. This only becomes possible by putting aside the daily distractions that clutter our minds. Author Robin Sharma refers to this as "the age of dramatic distraction."

Dreams are never right or wrong, they just are what they are. They are messages from our subconscious mind we could choose to take action on or not. It has been said that dreams without action are just illusions. This simply means that if your dream is compelling enough, you must take action or it will never be realized. Having a dream is step one, and taking action is step two. A great life philosophy to live by is to find those who have had a similar dream to yours, took action, found success, and achieved their dream. If you do the same things they do, you'll increase your own chances of success. We will discuss this further in Chapter Three, "Mentors."

To realize your dreams, it's important to your success to let go of the fear of judgment. It really doesn't matter what others think. It's your dream; therefore, the only thing that matters is what you think. Gandhi once wrote, "Never let someone walk with dirty shoes through the garden of your mind." Never allow the critics or the naysayers to pollute your mind with their own limited beliefs.

The thing about dreaming is, the clearer you are—with greater specificity and detail, using all of your senses—the more likely it is that your dream will become real. This is the process of visualization. When we visualize, the mind cannot tell the difference between an actual event and one vividly imagined in great detail. If you are able to engage all five senses so that within your mind's eye you can feel, taste, smell, hear, and see it, then your dream is already a reality. The greater the clarity in specificity of the dream, the greater the likelihood that you'll experience it. Your mind will believe it's already occurred, therefore, conspiring with every decision, thought, and action you have and moving you forward to make it your new reality. That's the beauty of dreaming; it reframes and reprograms the subconscious mind, which focuses on creation. The last, and arguably most important ingredient, is massive action. Don't discount the importance of taking massive action. There have been countless dreams that were never realized simply for lack of action. Dreams plus action equals a new reality.

Dreaming creates a new and higher vibrational tone and energy. The higher we vibrate, the more likely it is we are to attract our dream. Unfortunately, most people stop dreaming and, comparatively, experience low vibrational emotions such as fear, despair, depression, etc.—which only wind up attracting those low-tone energies and experiences. It's the reason we repeatedly attract the same type of experiences, people, places, and things in our lives. If we want something new and different, we need to act and think differently. There's no better place to start this process than by dreaming.

The Five Steps to Dreaming

Step number one: What's Possible?

Begin with a childlike heart by asking: what's possible? Honor your response; the bigger the better. Make note of it and don't diminish or minimize any thoughts or ideas.

Step number two: Your Happy Place

Find your place. You can dream anywhere, but typically most of us have a place that inspires us to think bolder.

Step number three: Eliminate the Naysayers

Eliminate all the people who don't support you. I don't mean anything drastic, but find a way to remove their influence from your life.

Step number four: Dream Builders

Surround yourself with people who support and empower your dreams. These could be mentors, coaches, or anyone interested in seeing your dream become a reality.

Step number five: Get Going

Take action; no dream can become a reality without taking bold action. Failure doesn't occur by taking action; it only happens if we never start, or we quit.

Eliminating the Obstacles to Dreaming

1. What previous thoughts or beliefs do you hold about dreams?

2. How would letting go of your old beliefs about dreaming serve you in a positive and productive way?

3. What would your life look like if you dreamed more regularly?

4. What date do you plan on implementing dreaming as a part of your success habits?

CHAPTER THREE
"MENTORS"

"I'm not a teacher, but an awakener."

~ ROBERT FROST

Early in my career, I was sitting in my office having a phone conversation with a prospective business consultant. Well, it wasn't really a conversation; it was more of a monologue of me expressing my frustrations with all the things that were going wrong within my business. I was complaining about staffing issues. We were losing employees as fast as we could hire them. However, my complaints were not limited to just employees, they were all-encompassing—covering literally anything and everything I could think of at the time. This monologue, which felt like hours on my end, probably lasted less than five minutes. At the conclusion, I actually felt better. I felt like I'd given the consultant everything he needed to figure out what was going wrong within the business.

After I finished, I waited for his response. There was this awkward silence that seemed like an eternity. Eventually, I asked, "Hello, are you still there?" and he said, "Yes." He then said, "I know what's wrong with your business." I emphatically responded, "Great, what is it?" While thinking to myself, *this is really going to be great, now I can move beyond all these troubles.* However, his exact words—which would ultimately rock my world—were, "Your business is waiting for a leader to show up." Hello, two by four to the head. I was like, *you have got to be kidding me. I just explained to you everything that was going wrong!* At which point he said, "Your problems are not outside, your problems are inside—inside of you. Businesses rise and fall on leadership and right now your business lacks leadership." Ouch! At that moment, you'd have thought somebody had taken a saw and cut me right in half. I felt hurt, humiliated, and angry, but you know what? He was exactly right.

~Humility~

It was my arrogance and hubris that had devolved our business into an endless series of problems. I thought I knew it all. I thought I could figure it out on my own. I didn't want to admit that I needed help. I lacked the humility necessary to learn what I needed to know to create the success I desired. The beginning of this chapter is about learning humility, because receiving mentoring requires immense humility. It's being humble enough to understand that you might not know everything. We need to be open-minded to the instruction and help of others. Being humble is not a weakness; it's actually a strength. For most of my life, I thought I knew it all and I didn't need anyone's help. This attitude in my business brought me to the brink of complete and utter frustration. I was so unhappy; I was even considering quitting and doing something different. Arrogance (and I was full of it) will blind you, rendering you incapable of seeing the solutions that might be at hand. Perhaps, more importantly, it'll make you incapable of seeing the people who can assist and help you to overcome any and every problem you'll face, in business or in life. Fortunately for me, I was finally open to hearing the words the consultant spoke to me.

Humility is acknowledging that you need help. The vast majority of successful people, in both business and in life, have the habit of seeking out mentors to assist them on their path to success. That willingness to not only seek out instruction, but to actually accept it, is one of the cornerstones of a successful life.

~*Curious Minds*~

Finding or attracting a mentor begins with the concept of a curious mind. A curious mind is one that is inquisitive, with a desire to learn and grow. It's amazing the type of people who will show up in your life when you have a desire to learn. The funny thing is, these mentors are most likely already present in your life. The development of the curious mind is what allows us to finally recognize how they might be able to help us.

This reminds me of a time back in college when I was studying for a big exam. It was late that evening, I was leaving the library and I walked past a lecture hall. I heard a familiar voice resonating from inside, so I decided to take a look. As I peeked inside, I was surprised to see Dr. Richard Rada, the first chiropractor who'd had a major influence on my life. As he was giving a lecture about chiropractic, I decided to sit down and listen. While he was explaining to the audience what chiropractic care was, I realized he was telling the same story he had told me just a few months prior. For whatever reason, I actually heard what he was saying this time, and I was blown away; so much so, it changed my life. At that moment, I decided to no longer pursue my education to become an orthopedic surgeon. Instead, I chose chiropractic as my profession.

The point is that most of us have probably had similar experiences. We have heard a message more than once, but didn't really hear it or pay attention to it until the right voice stimulated a curious mind within us. This curious mind, as discussed above, makes all the difference in our ability to learn and understand. It's like when we listen with an open heart, free of judgment and receptive to the message, is when we're ready to learn. This reminds me of one of my favorite quotes, "When the student is ready, the teacher will appear."

We must be in the right frame of mind with a readiness and receptiveness to grow. Learning requires humility — a willingness to admit that we don't have all the answers. When we tap into our humility, we are ready to receive the mentors that are all around us.

How do we sort through all the countless messages that we are bombarded by every day? Information comes from countless sources. Sifting through this noise and chaos is much easier when we have a trustworthy and respected voice to help us decipher and understand what it is we're hearing. Being able to trust is an important part of receiving mentoring. Without trust, there is no safe place in which a foundation of confidence can be built. It doesn't matter how great the mentoring is if we can't let go of fear and past programming. So, I guess you can say that mentoring requires some faith. To me, faith is believing without seeing, without any tangible evidence to support our belief. Not a blind faith, but a faith that you know to your core what you're hearing is true, right, and just. You can get all the best suggestions and ideas in the world but, without trust, you would never take action.

Letting go of the fear and uncertainty is an essential quality to being mentored. It truly is a leap of faith.

At some point, we must begin to trust if we are going to change and grow. Not everything that occurs in life is easily explainable. Some things happen without explanation. I like to think it is the universe conspiring with our hearts' intent. This is evidence that you're following your purpose. Trusting in the process is a leap of faith that will reward you in the end if you're willing to believe.

~Authenticity~

The beauty of true mentorship is that mentors often serve with no expectation of anything in return. They serve selflessly and from their heart. Contrary to popular opinion, there are people who want to serve and expect nothing in return. They really care about you and your success. The more authentic people we have in our lives, the more blessed we are. Authentic people walk their walk and talk their talk. They give us a feeling inside; a knowing that they do truly care about what is best for us. This is when you know that you've found the right person. I guess you can say this can also relate to having faith, but it doesn't take long to see the true authenticity of someone shine through—through their actions and words. Great mentors won't just tell you the way, but will show you the way. Therefore, once applied, you have a new skillset that is developed for a lifetime.

Once you've experienced the incredible benefits of being mentored, you'll most likely want to become a mentor yourself. As I've mentioned before, I've been blessed with many great mentors in my life. They have authentically given so much of themselves—their time, energy, and resources. These experiences compel me to pay it forward and help others. To reach out and assist others as they embark upon their path is my personal mission. To inspire others to help them live happier, healthier, and more prosperous lives. That is my mission, and I give thanks daily for the opportunity to live this mission. I am truly fortunate to be able to do this through my speaking, teaching, writing, consulting, and coaching. There is nothing more rewarding than serving others. There's no greater feeling than to help another person achieve their goals, to help them see a brighter future, and explore new opportunities that once were never imagined. Nothing will elevate your self-worth more than serving another human being.

Mentors come in all sizes and shapes, and they are all around us. They are friends, teachers, coaches, ministers, business leaders, authors, athletes, spouses, and parents—the list is almost endless. Mentors often show up at both the best and worst of times, whether we're ready or not. The most influential mentor in my life was my father-in-law, Dr. Joe Stucky. No one taught me more about being a professional, a caregiver, leader, and about unconditional love and service.. He lived by the axiom "To love, to give, to serve," and he did that so richly. He was a great example of this to me and countless others. He helped shape and mold me into the man that I've become, and the success that I've been able to achieve. My gratitude and appreciation is immense. He saw things in me that I never saw in myself. Just a few weeks before he passed away, I shared with him the story in which I was halfway through graduate school. I was completely out of money and was going to have to drop out of school. I had been dating his daughter (my wife now), Pam, roughly six months, and we were not even engaged at the time. Pam had told her parents of my dire financial situation. Through their generosity and belief in me, they paid for my semester of school. Think about that: they wrote a check because they believed in me and were willing to invest in me, expecting nothing in return except for the hope that one day I would pay it forward. I joked with my father-in-law that it was the best $2000 investment he ever made. We both chuckled and, with a quick wink, I knew he was in agreement.

Truth be told, the importance of this story really had very little to do with the money and everything to do with their belief in me. They gave me a chance and taught me about selflessness and generosity. That belief resulted in me recommitting and working harder than I'd ever done previously. You see, mentoring creates an accountability that will often provide a greater motivation than going it alone ever could.

When our life is nearing its end, this is how we'll be remembered — by the impact we made on the lives around us. Did we make our world a better place to live? Did we inspire others? Did we make a difference? Did we live a life well-served? There's no better way to make this possible than to have a mentor in our lives, or to become one ourselves.

How to find good mentors:

1. **Be receptive to potential mentors:** Be conscious of people who are an example of what you would like to become. With everyone that you come in contact, ask yourself, "Is this person living a life I wish to have? Do they exemplify the qualities and characteristics that I wish to learn?" Mentors can be found anywhere, so keep an open mind to the possibilities.

2. **Identifying potential mentors:** Make a list of those people you have identified. What are the qualities you admire of those on your list? This could be business savvy, integrity, confidence, financial success, strong relationships, or fitness—whatever the skill or quality it is you want to learn.

3. **Make the call:** This is when you may become the most uncomfortable. Call and invite your potential mentor out for lunch or coffee. Tell them that you want to pick their brain about... (and insert whatever you want to learn). Remember, this is where your humility needs to shine through. Asking for help is not a sign of weakness, but a sign of strength.

4. **Be specific:** At your meeting, have an outline ready. What skill or quality are you interested in learning? Be humble and share with them what it is you admire about them. Where did they learn this? Are there any resources they would recommend?

5. **Ask for help:** This may be the toughest of the steps. You'll definitely be stretched outside your comfort zone. Ask them if they'll help you. Don't be surprised if they're more than willing to do so. Mentors have a passion to serve others.

6. **Get to work:** Be ready to learn and take action. Your hard work and commitment is often more than enough of a payback to your mentor. If your mentoring requires a fee, understand you are making an investment in you for your future—it will pay off if you do the work. Remember to always give thanks and praise constantly for the help you're receiving.

7. **Pay it forward:** Look for the opportunity to help someone else on their journey. Become a mentor yourself.

Eliminating the Obstacles to Mentoring

1. What previous thoughts or beliefs do you hold about mentors?

2. How would letting go of your old beliefs about mentoring serve you in a more positive and productive manner?

3. What would your life look like if you had mentors?

4. What date do you plan on implementing mentorship as a part of your daily success habits?

CHAPTER FOUR
"AUTHENTICITY"

"Be yourself, there's no one else like you."

~ UNKNOWN

When I was in my twenties, there was a popular phrase, "Be real." It was a phrase that really meant, "Give it to me straight and no BS." It was quite popular for some time but, like many things, culture and times change. The slogan went out of favor, but the phrase "be real" is quite appropriate for this chapter. I used to reference this phrase quite frequently. In fact, I would use it interchangeably. Ironically, the more I would use this phrase, the more emptiness I would experience. That emptiness came from the fact that I didn't know who the real me was. As I got older and began to use more appropriate language, I found the term that resonated with "be real" was the word "authenticity." Authenticity defined means a genuineness, or being true to who we are. How many twenty somethings or, for that matter, people of any age are fortunate enough to really know who they are? In my own life, I consider the decade of my twenties as the decade of self-indulgence. I believed that the whole world revolved around me. As time passed, I realized that wasn't the case. So, in my thirties I began to explore the process of personal growth and self-awareness. Now mind you, you don't have to wait until you are in your thirties to figure this out. Perhaps I was just a slow learner. Getting to know who we are might be one of the most important things we ever experience. This process can be painful. It requires a lot of introspection, quiet time, and thought, but the rewards can be immeasurable.

Have you ever wondered why you believe what you believe? Have you bought into some old axioms like *money doesn't grow on trees, rich people are selfish and evil,* or even that *a woman's place is in the home?* I know many of these old sayings come from generations past but, nonetheless, they were beliefs passed on by people we trusted and loved. Our parents were simply passing on to us what was passed down to them from their parents. We must examine these ideas to assess whether they are a universal truth — like what goes up must come down — or just something we accepted without even thinking about it. As we discussed in this book on a few occasions, our thought and belief systems dictate our life's experiences. If we don't challenge our belief systems, then we're resigned to stay in a state of sameness. Have we really ever examined the beliefs we hold as it relates to finances, gender, race, culture, relationships, education, or sex — the list is nearly endless. Do they reflect our true beliefs or beliefs of others?

Taking stock of our belief systems in each of these areas will help us to begin to understand how we think, and why we act the way we do. Now, your current belief systems as you examine them might be appropriate. They may resonate quite deep within you, and there's no need to change them. However, if you spend little to no time examining your belief systems, it's a good bet that many of your belief systems don't reflect your authentic self. Therefore, you're currently just repeating the old belief systems that you were taught from the most influential people in your life: parents, grandparents, teachers, clergy, etc.

Growing up in a strong Italian family, I had the belief system that the best food in the world was Italian food. And although that may be true, that stopped me from experiencing and trying all kinds of different cultures and their food. For years, I never stepped outside of your typical fast food or Italian restaurants. I had no idea what I was missing, until one day we were invited to join friends for dinner at a Korean restaurant. The experience and the food were both wonderful. I thought to myself, *If Korean food is good, Japanese food must be just as good! What about French food, Mexican food, English food?* Well, maybe not perhaps the English food, if you've been to England. But the point is we can become so rigid in our thoughts and ideas that we never venture beyond what we already know. This prevents us from experiencing an infinite number of other thoughts and beliefs that might be integral to our future growth. That growth is necessary to expand our vision so we can better understand who we truly are.

Growing up, I often aspired to be like my heroes—such as a professional baseball player or rock star. Even though I enjoyed those passions, I did so without truly understanding what was important to me. There's a fine line between emulating the qualities and characteristics of someone you admire and giving up the uniqueness of who you are. We all have various strengths and weaknesses. We need to learn, understand, and embrace each of them. Most of us spend far too much time thinking and focusing on what we don't do well. Things that make us unique and different are the talents that we're really good at. I found more success by focusing my time and energy on my strengths.

Children, as well as many adults, are always looking for acceptance from outward sources, whether it be our parents, family, or friends. Only true acceptance comes from within. When we're young and emotionally fragile, the words of the most influential people in our lives can have a profound effect on our thoughts and belief systems. Even the most innocuous statement could leave a lasting scar on our subconscious mind as an impressionable child. For example, as a child, I was out playing basketball and one of the older kids (who I admired greatly as an athlete) said that I'd never be a good basketball player because I couldn't jump very high and, at the time, he was absolutely right. But what I heard was, *you're not a good athlete, you'll never be any good, so don't waste your time.* When I internalized that it became my reality which, in turn, became my belief system. For the longest time, I would never pick up a basketball because of this, even though this belief system is not rooted in any truth whatsoever. In fact, as I got older, I realized that I was actually a pretty decent athlete but, for the longest time, I would not challenge myself athletically because of that negative belief.

It's these kinds of comments and jabs, even in jest, that can unintentionally lead to low self-esteem and low self-worth. Those comments can have a huge influence, which can alter our internal belief system and how we view ourselves. One of the most common elements that people have trouble with is a lack of self-worth and self-love. A lack of self-worth leads to self-sabotage. Self-sabotage will often occur when we begin to make progress and self-improvement. We subconsciously undermine that progress to move us back to what is called an emotional set point. These are best described as our self-imposed comfort zones, stemming from beliefs such as, "I can't lose weight," or "I'll never become wealthy." Thoughts like these will sabotage any attempts made to change. The only way to overcome these set points is by changing our belief system. One of the best ways for doing so is by getting to our true authentic self.

When we begin to explore who we are—and I know this may sound crazy—we must fall in love with ourselves; not in a conceited, self-loathing manner, but one that honors and respects our uniqueness. The ironic thing is, until we fall in love with ourselves, it's impossible to love others. You see, you can't give away what you don't own. This means that unless we are love, we can't give love away. This is often evident in people who struggle with relationships, as they always seem to be attracted to people who are toxic for them. They tend to attract the same type of individual over and over. Our culture plays a big part in this; when you watch any sort of TV show or movie, read books and magazines, listen to the radio, or any type of advertisement or marketing, the overriding message tends to be that you're lacking something, and we (they) have what it is that you need. It might be that fancy new car to make you feel whole as a man, or the new pair of shoes and purse that will make you that attractive stunning woman. It might be that little pill to make you a voracious lover.

We are bombarded daily with thousands of messages telling us about how inadequate we are. If your psyche is fragile, you buy into this and start to look for external reasons to fill something that requires an inside solution. It creates an illusion that we're not whole, and we must search outside ourselves to find fulfillment. This is false programming, commercialism, materialism, alcohol, drugs, sex; all these forms of escapism only provide a temporary high to fill the void within. They create a neurochemical high which we become addicted to, requiring another shopping spree, another new car, the next drug or alcoholic beverage. This fuels the addiction cycle, which leads to a self-destructive pattern, all based on a set of lies. Each time we fill that emptiness, the high has to get stronger to fill the void as the void gets deeper. That void can pull us deeper into the inevitable outcome of an ultimate crash and burn. Truly understand that nothing from outside yourself can fulfill the void of inside yourself — that void is self-love. We must learn to love ourselves before we accept someone else into our life.

Most relationships fail because we're hoping that we can find the things that we believe we are lacking within ourselves from someone else. Unfortunately, no one can ever live up to that expectation. Eventually this will lead to disappointment and disillusionment in the relationship, ultimately leading to its demise. By learning who we are, and what makes us unique and different, we can embrace and learn to accept ourselves. The process of filling this void takes time, work, and can be painful, but it is truly the only solution to break this endless destructive cycle. We must first begin by understanding that happiness is an emotion and, like every emotion, our emotions are choices. Either we are in control of them or someone else is. Don't choose to be a victim. We can choose to be happy or sad, angry or calm, content or disappointed, fearful or faithful. This doesn't mean that bad things or things that upset you don't occur, because they do — life will always happen. It's how we choose to react to these life situations that matters. When living authentically, we have a better understanding of who we are and we can choose to focus on the negative or the positive. Keep in mind, within every negative experience is the seed of new opportunities.

The four steps to living authentically

Step number one: Examine your most deeply held beliefs about yourself and your surroundings. Are these beliefs your truths, or truths that you've accepted from others? If you reject the beliefs that you're currently holding, write out a new set of belief systems for yourself.

Step number two: Choose to focus on your strengths. Identify three to five of your strongest attributes. If you're having trouble identifying those attributes, ask someone close to you. They should share them with you freely. You should spend 80% of your time on the things you enjoy and are really good at.

Step number three: Choose the emotion and energy you want to live by. Prepare your mind in advance for when adversity and challenges in life occur. How will you choose to react? Will you choose despair, anger, disappointment, or regret, or will you choose optimism, hope, faith, and opportunity? Inherent in every negative is a positive. Do you choose to acknowledge that?

Step number four: Choose relationships that allow you to be you. The people who truly love you for who you are will celebrate you and not try to change you into something you're not, or someone they want you to be. True authenticity lies in the ability to live your life as you see fit; to follow the path that God has put you on to experience the most joy and happiness that your journey has to offer.

Eliminating the Obstacles to Living Authentically

1. Do you feel like you live true to your authentic self?

2. What previously held thoughts, behaviors or beliefs do you need to eliminate to live more authentically?

3. What would your life look like if you lived more authentically?

4. What date do you plan on implementing authentic living into your daily success habits?

CHAPTER FIVE
"GRATITUDE"

"Gratitude is not only the greatest of virtues,
but the parent of others."

~ CICERO

Who doesn't love the Pharrell song, "Happy"? It's nearly impossible to listen to that song and not bounce around, move, or dance. The energy, tone, and vibration of that song just makes you feel good about yourself.

How would you define happiness? Does happiness come from extraneous temporal experiences? Those momentary experiences that might occur from our purchasing a new pair of shoes, or perhaps buying the latest electronic gizmo we desire. Happiness can be when we're around the people we love. It could be a warm sunny day, or sitting by the ocean and listening to the waves rolling up on the shore. Happiness can be an easy Sunday morning or a wonderful meal with friends and family. Happiness can come in so many forms and so many variations. The cool thing is that we get to decide what it is that makes us happy. However, so many of the things I just mentioned are temporary; they're fleeting. Some experiences may leave you with a sense of emptiness shortly thereafter, resulting in the need for the next fix. This often leads to addictive types of behaviors, such as over-consumption of alcohol, medications, shopping, or unnecessary purchases. It has been my experience that true happiness occurs when we learn gratitude.

Gratitude is defined by Wikipedia as "a thankfulness, gratefulness, or an appreciation, a feeling or attitude, an acknowledgement of a benefit that has been received or will be received." To me, gratitude is being thankful for all things that exist in our lives, whether we considered them good or bad at the time. In every life experience there's an opportunity sewn within; a chance to experience something new or to be challenged, which will cause us to grow. Gratitude is an acknowledgement; an acceptance that all things currently present in our lives are there for a reason, and being thankful that they are present. Gratitude is also a consciousness of being thankful for things yet to come; for the things that we define as being good, as well as the things that we see as difficult. Many people come to gratitude when they experience a significant life challenge, such as a health issue with themselves or a close family member. If they're fortunate enough to overcome this obstacle, the overwhelming emotion experienced is gratitude. Gratitude to be able to overcome the health challenge, to experience a new outlook on life, to have a second chance, and this often leads to a new perspective on things that were perhaps once taken for granted. The simple small things in life we now acknowledge as being true blessings.

If you look back in your life, I would bet that some of the greatest experiences you've ever had were also your most trying times. They molded you into the person you've become. I have many examples of this in my own life. One, in particular, is when I was faced with a major health scare. At the time, I was in my early thirties with three small children when I developed a condition called Benign Fasciculation Syndrome. This is a condition that causes muscles to flutter and twitch. It can occur in a single muscle or throughout your entire body. Think of a million worms crawling all over your body. Not a pleasant experience. This condition began following the completion of my first triathlon, which seemed weird. Unfortunately, my condition was incessant and 24/7 nonstop. It being part familial and part stress-related, as well as the result of nutritional deficiency—which was the precipitating factor in my case. But as a healthcare provider, I knew that fasciculation is also associated with ALS or Lou Gehrig's disease. Before I was diagnosed with the benign form of this condition, I was terrified that I was going to die and leave my wife husbandless and children fatherless. All I wanted was a positive diagnosis. It was all I thought about for many weeks before my exam was completed and test results were known. At times, I felt helpless—like my life was on hold. I was also feeling completely overwhelmed, anxious, and depressed. I thought this couldn't be happening to me. I lived the right way. I did all the right things. I worked out, ate right, and didn't smoke. I lived a healthy lifestyle. I would have done anything to avoid the fate associated with this disease. Unfortunately, those families touched by this disease know, ultimately, this disease is a death sentence.

During the greatest challenge of my life, all I could think was, if I could get a second chance I would live my life differently. I prayed for that second chance. I would be a better dad, husband, and leader. I would be kinder and more grateful. Fortunately for me, on that fateful day, I got that second chance. The doctor told my wife and me it was not ALS and that I was not going to die. I was shocked, relieved, overjoyed, and immensely grateful. I couldn't believe the words coming from his mouth. My wife and I were in tears. I thanked God for the positive news. Believe me, my perspective on life changed forever. It wasn't that I didn't cherish my life before then, but going through something like that will change you—and it did change me in a big way. I had a much deeper sense of gratitude than ever before. I committed to the pledge I made to myself to be a better human being. Rather than looking at the world as the glass is half-empty, I now saw the world in a totally different light.

So, I ask the question, why is it that we don't live in a deep sense of gratitude all the time? Why is it that, often times, we need a tragedy to occur before we come to this realization? It is my hope through my experience that you can come to a conclusion without experiencing a major life challenge. The human condition is constantly looking at what's not right, rather than seeing all the good that exists. Because, if we choose to open our eyes and change our perspective, good does exist all around us. How do we get conditioned to be so negative all the time? Is it possible to change and, if so, what does it take? What are the steps?

Let's first start by understanding that gratitude has historically been a focus of most world religions. It reinforces present and future emotional and psychological benefactors. It has been found that those who appear or attend religious service more often are more likely to have a greater sense of gratitude in all areas of their lives.

A study was done that found a 70% increase in sales when customers of a jewelry store were called and thanked for their purchases, compared to customers who were not called. Servers at a restaurant who wrote "Thank you!" on the back of patrons' checks received bigger tips. A most recent, larger study found that people who are grateful experience a higher sense of well-being.

Grateful people are happier; they are less depressed, less stressed, and more satisfied with their lives and social relationships. That study was from the *Journal of Personality and Social Psychology*. That study also indicated that grateful people also have higher levels of control of their environment, personal growth, purpose in life, and self-acceptance. These are just a few of the examples and studies that have shown the positive effects of a consciousness of gratitude.

Gratitude, like any other emotion, is a choice. Each day or, for that matter, each moment, we get to choose the emotion that we want to experience. At this point you're thinking, *I already do*. But the reality is, most of the time we are reactionary with our emotions and not consciously choosing them. Therefore, we allow our circumstances and those around us to have the greatest influence on our emotions. So the question is, are we more influenced by external circumstances or internal thoughts?

Many people are stuck in the habit of complaining and criticizing rather than taking responsibility for their own thoughts and behaviors. Ultimately, this results in seeing yourself as a victim and in today's culture this is heavily reinforced. This creates a predicament that is nearly impossible to overcome. The most obvious example of this was the financial crisis of 2008, brought on by millions of people unable to pay mortgages because of the easy access to debt that had been made widely available. Neither the lenders nor the borrowers saw this as a problem until the bubble burst, resulting in the largest bank bailout in history. The Government created policies that encouraged predatory lending to people who couldn't afford the loans, while at the same time they threatened lenders if they failed to make those loans. The crazy thing is that no one took responsibility for the mess and chose to blame others for their incompetence. Who was left to pay the tab for the bad policies? Us — the tax payers.

The simplest way to overcome victimhood is to develop a strong sense of gratitude in your life. In fact, it is virtually impossible to be a victim and be grateful at the same time.

The exciting thing about gratitude is that it doesn't only benefit the one expressing the gratitude, but the individual receiving it also experiences a higher level of personal satisfaction. I guess what I'm trying to say very simply is, if you want to change your life, start by adding an attitude of gratitude. It's the simplest thing you can do to begin to change your outlook on life. In a sense, it will be like reprogramming your operating system of your subconscious mind. This helps us move away from being our old self with the old thoughts, beliefs, actions, and emotions we've had repetitively for years. If we want to choose a new experience, we have to begin by reprogramming the mind and, particularly, the subconscious mind from which 95% of all our actions originate. We're creatures of habit, and when we begin to move away from unconsciously producing thoughts, beliefs, actions, and emotions, to taking control more consciously — in other words, being more aware of those things — we begin to rewire the brain to fire differently. We then create new thoughts, new beliefs, new actions, new emotions, and new results.

This all starts with the consciousness of awareness. Being aware of the thoughts that we're experiencing all the time is so counterintuitive to today's culture and society. Virtually everything that we experience is designed to move us away from reality, to move us away from conscious thought, and to dull our senses — which results in a mind-numbing experience. Shifting our consciousness requires a reawakening to conscious living. So let me be clear; all we have to do is to remind our self who we no longer want to be. This may seem difficult and challenging, but it starts with a simple decision, one in which you begin by asking a question. *Do I choose to continue to experience the life I have, or do I want something new and different?* If your answer is the latter, then let's begin by changing our thoughts so we anchor ourselves to a consciousness of gratitude.

The interesting thing about rewiring the mind is that once you create your new habit and behavior (i.e., your new self), it's impossible to have two opposing thoughts at the same time. So when you're in a consciousness of gratitude, you are less likely to experience things like hatred, anger, and fear. The more we focus on what's good, the more we attract what's good. This is not a simple play on words, but one that I've experienced on countless occasions. For example, I had a desire to serve more people in our community. To do so, I needed to share with them the life-changing benefits of natural healthcare and chiropractic. This could provide my community with more abundant health and vitality, so I began to express more gratitude for the opportunity to serve. The funny thing is, the more gratitude I expressed, the faster my business grew. The more I focused on it each day, the busier I got, and the more patients I started to see. The act of being truly grateful built my business.

I can give you countless other examples of similar experiences, but this is why I have such a strong belief that gratitude is a foundation that can change your life, and the lives of those around you, for the better. Gratitude unlocks the power of abundance, which attracts things to us by first giving thanks for what it is you want to create ahead of time. There's no greater source and no greater tool to start with than gratitude. It will make the world around you a better place to be, inside and out.

The six steps to create more gratitude in your life.

Step number one: Create a gratitude journal. One can be purchased at the store, or you can simply use a loose-leaf notebook or a journal/notebook app on your mobile device.

Step number two: Write down all the things that you're currently thankful for in your life; all the things that are going well. This could be your health, relationships, job, finances, or friends. List them all as completely and as thoroughly as possible.

Step number three: List and identify all the current challenges you're experiencing in your life. For example, you might be experiencing challenges with your family, relationships, health, career, etc. Be as thorough as possible. The second part of this step is to answer the question, *How does this current challenge benefit me in my life? What lessons am I supposed to learn from this experience?* This can be a difficult step, but give this serious thought. *In what ways will this challenge make me stronger?* List each one as thoroughly and completely as possible. I want you to see the inherent opportunity, and the lesson, from each of these challenges. This will begin your mental reframing.

Step number four: At the conclusion of each day, open your gratitude journal and date it, then write out three things that you're currently grateful for on that particular day. These can be as simple as a home-cooked meal, beautiful rain on a spring afternoon, or a new book you started to read (hopefully mine). Then write one challenge you had for that day, why you're thankful for it, and what you learned from it. The power from this habit is nearly immeasurable. This literally begins to retrain your brain by neurologically rewiring how the brain fires into a habit of thinking in a gratitude consciousness.

Step number five: Each morning upon waking, before you even open your eyes, give thanks for another opportunity to live your dream. Give thanks for the abundance in your life, for your health, your family, and your ability to serve and to live out your dream, and for the one big goal you want to accomplish that day. This will begin the flow of gratitude in your consciousness as you start your day.

Step number six: Do each of these lessons every day and without fail. In the beginning, creating these new habits can be a challenge. The more diligent and consistent you are with applying these steps daily, the faster you'll create the new habit of gratitude. Before long, if you keep at it, you'll begin to receive all the amazing benefits of gratitude in all aspects of your life.

Eliminating the Obstacles to Create More Gratitude

1. What dominant emotion (fear, uncertainty, doubt, anger, envy, guilt or despair) do you need to release to live presently in gratitude?

2. How will living in a state of gratitude change your life?

3. What would your life look like if you lived in the presence of gratitude?

4. What date do you plan on implementing gratitude into your daily success habits?

CHAPTER SIX
"VALUES"

"It's not hard to make a decision when you know what your values are."

~ ROY DISNEY

Have you ever felt lost, directionless or lacking a sense of purpose in your life? This could be a sign or a symptom of being out of balance with your values or, more importantly, not being aware of your values. I've experienced this feeling myself on numerous occasions. The first I can recall was when I was a teenager at a family holiday. In fact, it was Thanksgiving and an uncle asked me what I was planning on doing for a career. I was 15 at the time, and I drew a blank. I kind of thought I knew, but I really had no specific idea or an understanding of what it was that I wanted to do.

The next occurrence was when I began college. I was taking general studies with an undeclared major, because I didn't know what I wanted to do or what my purpose was at the time. I was directionless. Like most students, I was hoping college would help me find my path.

Maybe you've had similar feelings. I think, at some point, most of us have had this happen to us. Unfortunately, for many people, they never identify with what their life's purpose is. Perhaps, for yourself, you might be working a job that you feel just doesn't fulfill you and you feel lost and frustrated. You're there simply to make a living and you have an emptiness inside knowing that there could be something more. Whatever the reason you may be having these feelings is directly tied to a lack of understanding or knowing what your values are.

Clearly defined values are the roadmap that creates our destiny. Values are that lighthouse in the storm. They provide a compass for our life, particularly during times of uncertainty, doubt, and fear. Some values are inherent, such as love, the need to be loved, to love others, as well as survival, or safety. These are inherent human values that we all experience. Other values are learned or developed over time. This can be a passion for travel, music, or art. It could be a desire to write a book. Whatever it is, defining your values is an essential tool to living a life of purpose and meaning, which can help you achieve your sense of peace.

Values exist whether we recognize them or not. Every decision and choice we make reflects our value system. The choices could reflect whether we get married or not, have children, where we live, the careers we choose, or simply to be generous or benevolent. Perhaps this is a good place to start. Defining your values often begins with understanding what's important to you and what matters the most. The number one source of stress in our lives is living incongruently with our values. Let that sink in. We all experience stress, but the greatest source of stress is when we're out of balance with our values. The effects of making choices that are incompatible with values have a significant toll on our mental, physical, and spiritual well-being.

There was a time, early in my practice, that I can remember when I was living inconsistent with my values. I was working 12-hour days, getting home late at night and, oftentimes, missing dinner and bedtime with my children and wife. This created a lot of internal conflict for me. I was feeling stressed out and unhappy because I was missing those important times with my family. Missing those informative times with my kids was really weighing heavily on me, and was beginning to affect my relationship with both them and my wife. I was more concerned about growing my business and paying off student loans, as well as providing a home for my family, than being present for my family. I was totally out of balance. An incongruence in my life. I clearly had to make a change or this was going to have a significant and lasting negative impact. I was putting money ahead of family. Talk about being off track? So, I made a decision to change, which allowed me to be home with my family early enough in the evening to enjoy dinner and reading to my children before bed. These times and activities were very important to me because I missed them with my father growing up. I wasn't going to allow my children to miss those important moments with me. Initially, this seemed like a difficult thing to do. However, it quickly became apparent that having that extra time with my family was directly in line with my values. The funny thing is that when I made this change, I experienced more happiness and balance, which resulted in more growth in my business. One of life's paradoxes.

At that time, family was number one on my values list. For most people, family is usually in their top five values. The interesting thing is values can change from year to year based on our priorities and the stages of life we are in. Early on when my children were young, family was the top priority. Now, as my kids are grown, family is still very important, but that value isn't as high because my children no longer live at home and are pursuing their own dreams.

Defining your values is not hard, but initially it can be challenging. I recall a time when I was working with a client who was successful in business, but was feeling unfulfilled. We began to explore where the lack of fulfillment was coming from, so we started with the process of defining his values. Of all the tools that I've used in my career in assisting others to achieve their goals, I've found this process to be one of the most powerful. Upon completion of defining his values, my client realized that his passion and his value system were different than the life that he was living. Even in the face of the immense success that he was experiencing, he decided to make a dramatic shift in his life. Many thought he was crazy. Why would he leave such a successful business to pursue something totally different? Those who don't understand the power of having clearly defined values would feel this way. But to my client, the choice was clear. He sold his business and pursued his dream as a writer. He never looked back. For him, the process and discovery was hard. It requires brutal honesty that can be difficult but oh-so-fulfilling on the other side. Usually, defining values will awaken people, making them more aware of the things that truly matter the most to them.

Assessing your values needs to be done annually. The best time is typically the fourth quarter, towards the end of the year, sometime in November or December. As you begin to set your goals for the upcoming year, defining your values first will provide you the foundation which is necessary to understand what goals you would like to accomplish. When I began to implement this process in my own life, I saw a dramatic shift in goal-setting and goal achieving. Prior to learning this process, I would become seduced by the goals of others and adopt them myself because they sounded cool. More often than not, I found that to be an exercise in futility. Adopting someone else's goals without also assessing how they relate to your values will almost never work. If you've found yourself in the past setting goals and not achieving them, it's probably because you've missed this important step.

To change your destiny, we must begin by identifying our values. Remember, values become your GPS for success. Without clearly-defined values, we're traveling down a road without a map. In fact, without the right vehicle to even get you there. Is it any wonder we never arrive to our destination?

Let's explore the steps to identifying values.

Defining values is a five-step process.

Step One: Begins with a simple question; what matters the most in your life? Before asking this question, get into a place or environment that provides a comfortable and relaxing atmosphere. This enhances the ability to clear your mind, which will allow you to get into a flow of creative consciousness. Limit external distractions, then begin with the question, *what matters the most in my life?* Sit quietly and reflect on your thoughts and see what comes to mind. Some examples might be family, health, financial freedom, fitness, travel, or being debt-free—the list is endless. (See Appendix – Values.) Then allow those words to flow onto paper. Write each word down that comes to mind. For most people, there should be between 40 and 60 different values. Don't judge your answers, just write them down. There's no right or wrong answer.

Step Two: Condense your values list into your top 10. Be sure to take some time to review, because you need to be certain of your choices.

Step Three: Is prioritizing your top 10 from most to least important. For many folks, family might be number one, and perhaps faith is number two. What matters most is your priority of values is accurately reflected.

Step Four: Once you have your values listed in order, take time to review this list daily over the course of three days. The order in which you have set them may change. Reviewing it frequently will create more clarity of the order in which your values should be.

Step Five: Involves rating your values on a scale of zero to 10, with 10 being living 100% consistent with that value, and zero meaning the opposite. This is a critical step in the process, because it requires you to be brutally honest with yourself. For example, if health is a really important value to you, but you have not spent any time exercising, eating well, getting proper rest, and you are 50 pounds overweight, then you're more of a one or two in the value of health. You'll want to apply this level of honesty with each value you are measuring.

Congratulations, now that you have completed this process, you have the foundation to ensure that your values are consistent with your goals. This greatly improves the likelihood of success in achieving all of your future goals. You'll experience greater certainty, which will help attract more success in your life. When our decisions align with our values, our purpose becomes clear, and life becomes magical.

Eliminate the Obstacles to Defining Values

1. What thought or belief do you hold that would prevent you from assessing your values?

2. What advantage would you have by identifying your values?

3. What would your life look like if you had clearly defined values?

4. What date will you complete and define your values and implement them into your daily success habits?

CHAPTER SEVEN
"MEDITATION"

*"To understand the immeasurable the mind
must be extraordinarily quiet, still."*

~ TIDDU KRISHNA MURTI

Have you ever had the experience where it seems like life is out of control? You're trying to juggle what seems like 1000 different things at one time: raising a family, growing a career, maintaining your health and finances — the list seems to never end. Like you, I've had this experience on numerous occasions as well, but perhaps no worse than in 1991. I had just joined my first practice. That same year, my wife Pam and I were blessed to have a second child, our son Anthony. At the same time, I was training for my first biathlon while working long hours at the office.

I remember going into the office one day, just not feeling right. I was anxious and out of sorts. It was about mid-morning on a beautiful spring day and I was seeing patients when I suddenly felt a tightness in my chest. My heart began to race and I started to feel clammy and sweaty. I had no idea what was going on; in fact, it was kind of like an out-of-body experience. I could see myself going through this, while simultaneously having a conversation. It was an odd and eerie experience. I thought this would go away, but it only progressed and got worse. I started to think that I was potentially having a heart attack, which would be awfully unusual for a 27 year-old that was in excellent shape. I couldn't understand what was going on. I felt like running out of the room. In fact, I couldn't get out of that treatment room fast enough. Upon completion of the visit, I literally ran outside trying to catch my breath. I thought, *should I go to the hospital? Who should I tell? Am I losing my mind?* All these negative thoughts were flooding my brain. Thankfully, the sensations started to dissipate. Through deep breathing and trying to refocus my mind, I was able to calm myself down. Unfortunately, that was only the first of many of these experiences.

I was soon to find out that this experience was known as panic attacks. I'd never experienced one and was not that familiar with them. I began to investigate what was the cause. Scientific literature at the time didn't really have much in the way of causation. As I began to dig deeper, I found that anxiety and panic attacks seemed to happen often for people who were dealing with a lot of stress — and I certainly was dealing with a lot of stress. I found out later that anxiety or panic attacks are merely a physical manifestation of unresolved emotional or physical stress. I didn't learn this in the medical literature, but through my own experience and personal research.

To rule out any physical cause, I went and saw a doctor who did a complete workup and found out that I was as healthy as could be. There was no underlying disease evident.

Being a person who takes action, I realized I was going to have to find out on my own how to deal with this issue. Knowing that it wasn't a physical problem, I knew the problem had to be psychological. It's hard to admit you may be losing your marbles. I don't mean to offend anyone who perhaps is currently experiencing this problem but, when you're going through panic attacks, it can certainly feel like you're losing it. My research revealed on more than one occasion that one of the best tools to get panic attacks under control is a process called meditation. The Tibetan word for meditation is *gom*, which means to become familiar with oneself. When you're young and healthy, you feel invincible. You feel like you can take on the world. Naturally, this is an illusion, a defense mechanism which causes us to not face our current reality or life struggles. Basically, we're on autopilot. Each and every day we are repeating the same habits and behaviors and living our lives trying to get ahead.

I realized I didn't really know who I was. The physical manifestations for the symptoms that I was experiencing were a reflection of my physical body telling me I wasn't right emotionally. The turning point occurred one day when I was in a Borders bookstore with my wife. We were searching for a book for our daughter's third birthday. I came upon the self-help section in the bookstore and something spoke to me. Something said "stop and take a look." The first thing I came upon was a cassette (more on that in a minute) by Dr. Deepak Chopra on meditation. I don't know why, but somewhere deep inside me, a voice was telling me I needed to purchase this—so I did. If you're like me, often after you purchase a book or CD, you put it on your desk and it could be weeks or months before you get to it, if ever. This time was different, though. When I got home, I immediately unwrapped the cassette. Yes, I said cassette—mind you this was 1991 and before the advent of MP3 players, cell phones, and all the great technology we have today. I put it in my Walkman (don't laugh) and I turned it on. I knew immediately upon hearing the lessons being taught that this was the secret sauce to help me deal with my problem.

I had started to do some extensive research on the physical and emotional benefits of meditation. Being a chiropractor and a wellness specialist, I wanted to know the ins and outs of how it worked, and were there any studies to support its effectiveness. What I found out was amazing. Here is what I learned:

Meditation has been proven to lower blood pressure, help with depression, and anxiety—and boy did I need help with that. It also helps people sleep better, improves memory, slows the aging process, boosts longevity, and helps people beat addiction. What was not to like? I was all in. One of my personal strengths is that once I commit to something, I'm all in! I began to practice daily the art of meditation. It has been said that prayer is when you speak to God; meditation is when God speaks to you. That hit me like a two by four to the head. It began to all make sense. I was really out of balance. My life had become so busy that I had stopped practicing my faith. I stopped listening to the voice within. I stopped dreaming. I was so busy being busy, I never took time to just…be.

Being a Type-A personality and going 1000 miles an hour all day every day is a recipe for physical and emotional disaster. I was experiencing it, and I was living it. Once I began meditating regularly, I began to notice a sense of relaxation, calmness, and a mindfulness that I had never experienced before. The interesting thing was, it wasn't just me. The people who were the closest around me began to notice a shift in me as well. Over time, I began to experience a greater sense of well-being. All the negative thoughts and emotions that I was experiencing, like anger, jealousy, and fear, became less powerful in my mind. I began to become more aware of my thoughts, emotions and feelings; where they were coming from and what was triggering them. For the first time in a long time, I felt like I was getting back on my path. As I practiced even more regularly over time, I began to notice that meditation allowed me to start to bring forward the things that I really and truly desired. Many experts say it's because we create a higher level of consciousness when we're in a meditative state.

The best way to describe meditation is it's kind of like that state you're in just prior to falling asleep. For those of you that are not aware, the brain operates in a number of different bandwidths or frequencies, usually referred to as cycles per second. This is essentially a measurement of your level of brain activity. Within these measurements are specific waves that have individual classifications. I believe a brief description of the four waves that we experience is important in the understanding of meditation.

The four types of waves begin with beta waves. Beta waves occur at 15 to 30 wave cycles per second, and we are generally most alert, awake, and most dominant when we're in beta. This is when we are motivated the most and have increased energy and focus. High levels of beta waves may lead to increased stress.

The next phase is alpha waves. These are 9 to 14 wave cycles per second. These waves are dominant waves during meditation when we are relaxed. An example would be when we have kind of a wandering mind, or a sense of relaxation. Meditation starts at this level. Increasing our alpha waves helps us become more creative, with less stress and an increased ability to heal.

The next wavelength is theta waves, which is 4 to 8 wave cycles per second. This is associated with deep meditation and hypnosis. This occurs during the twilight zone just between consciousness and sleep. You may get a sense of floating. Increased theta waves develop a greater sense of emotional awareness, along with advanced creativity and learning.

The fourth wave is known as delta waves, which are 1 to 3 wave cycles per second. This is the slowest of brain waves and occurs during very deep sleep. This is when our cortisol levels are decreased, which is a stress hormone. Increased cortisol can lead to advanced aging, chronic inflammation, and is a precursor to many chronic diseases.

My intention is not to make any of you scientists, but to help you understand that simply moving through these four wavelengths has a profound effect on our health and well-being—both mentally and physically. When we're in theta, our thoughts slow down and our minds become clearer. This can create a deep sense of purpose; a mental picture or image, if you will, of what you want your life to be. Another description of this would be visualization.

Meditation can be a struggle for some; it certainly was for me, initially. When we haven't cleared out the reservoir of our mind, we will often experience a cluster of thoughts racing through our mind. This is very common. It's the persistent practice of meditation over time that will help you gain control of these thoughts and get into theta; to slow the cycles of the brain down to reduce the amount of thoughts you're having. This is the sweet spot. This is when you enter the zone of peace.

The zone of peace is the ultimate destination with meditation. Your world slows down and the sense of fulfillment and happiness flows abundantly, with a calmness and clarity previously never experienced. The sustained practice and focus of meditation will help you achieve this desired state of mind. One in which you can go to any time you desire. Here are the steps.

Below are some recommended steps to beginning meditation in your own life.

Step one: Meditation should be done daily. You should find a comfortable location where you feel relaxed and at ease with no distractions. This may be indoors or outdoors. You may have soothing music playing or not. You may have the lights on or off. This is really based on your preference.

Step two: Find a comfortable chair, which you can sit in an upright position with your feet on the floor. Having the feet, preferably bare, grounded on the floor is a very important part of the process. Sitting in the upright position helps open up the diaphragm so you can breathe fully. Some may prefer to sit on the floor, which is entirely fine. I don't recommend lying down.

Step three: Start taking deep breaths in through your nose and exhaling out through your mouth, focusing on the breath in and out for 10 cycles. Once you've completed this cycle, the next part of this phase is to continue to breathe deeply into your nose, for a count of four, then holding for a count of eight, and exhaling out through the mouth for a count of 10, each time focusing on your breath. It will not be uncommon to experience a flood of thoughts that may seem random; do not fight this, simply refocus your thoughts back on your breath. Like any new skill, it will take some time to begin to focus solely on your breaths and eliminate any unwanted thoughts. Upon completion of step three, you should have a sense of calmness, perhaps a deep relaxation like one you've never experienced before—even a euphoric feeling. Your mind will seem clearer. Once your thoughts have slowed down, now it's time to begin the real fun.

Step four: Begin to visualize yourself, the new version of you, perhaps in a new job or in a new relationship. It could be a healthier version of yourself. You could also ask yourself, *who could I be? Who could I become if I removed all self-imposed limitations?* Begin to listen to the thoughts, the dialogue that begins to happen from within. This stokes the fire of what's possible. This process can take a few minutes or 20 minutes. There is no perfect amount of time to meditate. Some days if you only meditate five minutes, be grateful for it. If you can meditate 20 minutes, that would be fine as well.

As you begin implementing this new success habit, cut yourself some slack if you miss a day or two. It takes up to six weeks to create a new habit or behavior. The most important thing is to be aware of your thoughts. Observe the thoughts that you're having and the feelings that you're experiencing with it. Don't fight it— let it happen naturally. It's your inner voice beginning to speak to you once again.

Eliminate the Obstacles to Meditation

1. What thought or limiting beliefs do you have that would prevent you from meditating?

2. How would letting go of your old beliefs about meditation serve you in a positive and productive way?

3. What would your life look like if you meditated regularly?

4. What date do you plan on implementing meditation into your daily success habits?

CHAPTER EIGHT
"AFFIRMATIONS"

*"Affirmations are our mental vitamins,
providing the supplementary positive
thoughts we need to balance the barrage
of negative thoughts we experience daily."*

~ TIA WALKER

The whole process of personal transformation is about letting go of ego and getting to the very core essence of who you are. It's the person who you think you should be, not based on the ideas of society or the concepts of the people around you. Dr. Wayne Dyer once stated that, "Ego means excluding God out." It's not just about getting to who we really are and what really motivates us, it's also about unmasking the veil that we've put upon ourselves to create a persona, a falsehood, of who we think we should be or who we've chosen to portray to others. The pure joy and wonderment of life comes when we get to know who we are. This whole book is designed to help remove that veil to unlock your deepest-seated beliefs. To allow your true self to shine through, which will allow you to realize your full potential. Fulfilling your destiny.

It will be impossible to reach our potential if we allow ourselves to be judged by who society thinks we should be. It is far more important for us to choose who we desire to become. I believe you can take a quantum leap in this process by applying the next principle into the success habits of your life. That principle is called affirmations. An affirmation is a declaration, statement, or phrase which you repeat to yourself that defines your future intentions. This process, for most of us, is not new. Although what most people do is unintentional, such as negative self-talk, like, *I'm not smart enough...I'm not attractive enough...I'm too fat...I'm too skinny,* etc. So if you think about it, there isn't a day that goes by that we're not affirming something to ourselves. Sadly enough, the majority of those affirmations are negative.

As a child, we're being affirmed to all the time by our parents, teachers, and people of influence. We were told things such as *our family has always been poor and you'll be too. You're too slow to be a good athlete. You'll never amount to anything.* If you think about it, there are countless examples of statements like these from our past. Upon hearing those statements, we often accept them to be our truth and, unfortunately, as kids and even many adults, we don't have the intellectual capacity or understanding to challenge these beliefs. Why should we question them, aren't they being shared with us by people we love and trust? Most likely everyone has experienced this and, if you've ever been a parent, you've said things that you have regretted. That isn't to say necessarily that you had bad parents or bad role models, but to simply acknowledge behavior that occurs far too regularly and is greatly misunderstood. Keep in mind that our parents, teachers, coaches, and friends were usually well-meaning. However, they were often just repeating the same negative messages they were taught themselves — which is often the reason why we have a negative self-image in the first place.

Science has shown that our subconscious mind remains dominant from the time of birth up to the age of 12. What this means is that everything we hear, see, and experience goes directly into the deepest parts of our brain, thus making an indelible impression. This becomes a foundation of our personality, thoughts, actions, and beliefs before we even enter adolescence. What this proves is just how important a child's environment and influences are during the most critical phases of brain development.

One of the only ways to counteract all of this negative programming is to begin utilizing the power of affirmations. When we begin to implement the process of affirmation into our own lives, we begin to empower our dreams and ambitions to become our new reality. The empowering words of your affirmations provide a confidence and assuredness that we are on the right journey.

Affirmations have been proven to be effective due to their ability to rewire the brain. As the brain fires, it wires—which means as we change our thoughts, our brains begin to fire differently, creating new neural synapses. This, in turn, creates new brain pathways and their associated neurochemicals. I can't emphasize enough how much of a game changer this is. Once the process of affirmations and all the other habits in this book are a part of your day, like brushing your teeth, you are never the same. Rewiring of the brain means we look at the world differently. Our first response is no longer one of negativity, but of optimism, hope, and belief that you can accomplish anything. The old negative thought patterns are broken. The negative programming of the subconscious mind is short-circuited. Our view of the world is never the same. When we reach this point, we have accomplished the goal of changing our mind. Changing our destiny is sure to follow.

If this doesn't causes us to feel better about who we are, I don't know what will. Over time, these new synapses can transform the most negative person amongst us into the most positive people you know. My own life serves as an example of how successful affirmations can be.

Affirmations helped me change my very negative and fatalistic mindset that was created as a child. Early in life, I grew up in a pretty toxic environment. My siblings and I experienced the effects of a very ugly and nasty divorce. This resulted in a lot of anger and negative emotions. For me, I internalized this and felt responsible for the break up. This lead to a very poor self-image. I carried a lot of anger, plus I was incredibly negative. Affirmations played a key role in changing this mindset. My wife would confirm the level of negativity I had when we first met. It must have been my boyish good looks that attracted her to me, because it wasn't my attitude. I am thankful she stood by me as I worked hard on changing my negative head space. She tells me she married potential.

Affirmations can also have a positive effect not unlike exercise. After your affirmation, there is an increase in the feel-good chemicals in our brains, which are serotonin, dopamine, epinephrine, and norepinephrine. These are chemicals of the brain which make us feel happy, satisfied, loving, and grateful, with an overall general sense of well-being. Not only does it make you mentally feel good, but it also has a significant impact on your physical well-being as far as reducing heart rate, respirations, and blood pressure. It also naturally reduces anxiety and depression. You'll begin to notice an improvement in mood and disposition with a far more optimistic view of your life and future. So, if we accept the universal law that thoughts plus actions create reality, then affirmations play a vital role in disrupting, and eventually breaking, the patterns of our negative thoughts and actions which have ultimately undermined our success.

As I've mentioned many times, words have energy. They are either positive or negative, energizing or causing us to run out of fuel quickly. Remember simple chemistry; like attracts like, and opposites repel. Think about it. As you become more positive, your energy, mood, and whole outlook on life improves. Don't be surprised if those around you begin to notice this and you begin to attract more positive relationships. If your environment is stuck in toxicity and negativity, I know of no better way to change that experience than to learn that talking to yourself (positively) is not crazy. It's actually really good for you.

There are eight steps for writing effective affirmations. These steps are how highly successful people, teams, and organizations achieve success. You can change your life outlook by changing the picture you put inside your mind.

The eight steps to learn how to affirm:

Step number one: Affirmations need to be personal. They must begin with "I." You only can affirm for yourself. "I am" activates the personalization of each statement that allows you to take responsibility for the changes you want to make. This helps affirm your future outcome.

Step number two: Always be positive when describing what you want to affirm, what you want to attract, and what you're moving toward—not what you are moving away from. For example, "I am not fat" is an improper affirmation, whereas "I am losing weight easily" is more effective.

Step number three: Always include action words in your affirmations. These are descriptive words such as easily, quickly, rapidly, energetically, and confidently. This will move your mind to take action. An example would be, "I am easily attracting great relationships that nourish and fulfill me."

Step number four: Your affirmations should be in the present tense, as if they are happening right now. This requires using your own imagination. Over time, this will become easier with practice.

Step number five: Do not compare yourself to others, as this is never an effective tool or technique for affirming. Only measure your progress to yourself.

Step number six: Use words that emotionally resonate with you. The more emotion you feel while reading your affirmations, the faster the affirmation will become reality. It has been said that it is emotion that unlocks the trap door from the conscious to the subconscious mind.

Step number seven: Write affirmations for each area of your life. It is likely you have negative thoughts or limiting beliefs in each of the seven key areas. In the internationally bestselling book, *Oola: Find Balance in an Unbalanced World*, these seven areas are defined as faith, family, friends, fitness, field, finances, and fun. Write individual affirmations for each one of these important areas.

Step number eight: Review affirmations daily. Affirmations are best done early in the morning when the mind is clear and free of mental clutter. They should be reviewed multiple times, if possible—especially whenever negative thoughts rear their ugly head. For example, you can repeat your affirmations after you wake up, while in the shower, or on the way to work or school. Always state your affirmations out loud with energy, enthusiasm, and emotion. Most importantly, do this daily.

Step number eight (a): Whenever negative thoughts appear, review your affirmations.

Step number eight (b): Whenever negative thoughts appear, see steps eight and eight (a).

Eliminating the Obstacles to Affirmations

1. What limiting beliefs or fears do you hold about affirmations?

2. What limiting beliefs about yourself would you like to eliminate by practicing daily affirmations?

3. What would your life look like if you practiced daily affirmations?

4. What date do you plan on implementing affirmations into you daily success habits?

CHAPTER NINE

"BECOMING A GOAL SLAYER"

*"If you don't know where you're going,
you'll wind up someplace else."*

~ YOGI BERRA

I was in my early teens when I first heard about the process of setting goals. I believe I was 18 and reading Napoleon Hill's book *Think & Grow Rich*. I saw it in the library at school one day and I was drawn to it. I didn't know why—I couldn't explain it—but something deep inside me said, *you gotta read this book!* Now keep in mind this was not the norm for me. As a student, I certainly wasn't considered the most studious. In fact, the only books I ever read were the ones that were required reading, and even then I'd check out the Cliff Notes. But this time it was different, and so began my journey into self-discovery and learning about the habits, actions, and behaviors of success.

The lesson I took from that transformational book, which by the way is one of the most successful personal development books in the history of personal development books, is that in order to achieve, one must dream. Dreaming requires clarity, clarity inspires action, and action creates results. It all sounded good, but at the time I didn't quite understand what it meant—certainly not as a high school senior.

I understood the goal-setting portion of it, but didn't quite understand how significant the role of taking action was. In the 30 plus years since I read that book, I've discovered that there are more possibilities and opportunities than ever before to reach our human potential. Most of us feel overwhelmed with too much to do and the feeling of not enough time, when in reality we are all given the same amount of time. We are all affected by the same constraints of time, such as 86400 seconds or 1440 minutes in a 24-hour day, which totals 168 hours in a week. So, why is it some of us can be so productive and achieve so much in the same allotted time, when others can barely find enough time to work, take care of the home, pay the bills, and mow the lawn? What I discovered was simple but elegant. Those who are successful are extremely well-organized and focused on the most productive behaviors in their life, and those who aren't are stuck in the tedious actions and behaviors that consume their time with idle distraction.

Consider if you get home from work at 6 in the evening, make dinner, clean up, get ready for bed, and sit down to watch two hours of television. If you do that seven days a week, that's 14 hours a week of lost productivity. If you were like me, I would get up just minutes before I needed to leave the house, rush around take a shower, scarf some food down, and get to work or class five minutes late. What if instead of getting up at 7:30 to leave the house at 8, you got up at 6 and gave yourself an additional 90 minutes per day — an extra 10 and a half hours per week. With the 14 hours saved watching TV, we're already up to one additional day per week to increase your productivity and focus on important productive tasks. The key is becoming selective in what we choose to do and identifying the most important tasks that give us the best results.

As I struggled becoming productive myself, I began to realize that it was because I lacked clarity and, because I lacked clarity, I was without a plan. You could interchange the word plan with clearly-defined goals. I used to make goals for myself all the time and never wrote them down. I would just have them inside my head, as I figured that was more than enough. So each year I would make new goals for myself only to find out at the end of the following year I achieved very little, if any, of the goals I had made. Why was that? Is the process of goal-setting hogwash? I found that there was an additional aspect of goal-setting which was just as important, if not more important, than the actual goal itself. That process included writing down the goals; classifying them in the seven areas of life with specific action plans or action steps that are designed to help you achieve that goal within a specific timeline.

What quickly became evident was that, prior to learning this process, simply stating a goal was like having a wish. Unless it's written down, a goal doesn't really exist. So, the next step into changing your life is the process of goal-setting. A remarkable fact is only 3% of adults have clearly-defined written goals. These people are 5 to 10 times more likely to accomplish their goals when compared to people who are better educated. This proves that success is not merely for those of us who are the most educated, but for those who have clearly defined goals.

I believe the number one reason for procrastination is a lack of clearly-defined goals. Goals become our road map or, as I mentioned before, your GPS for life. Without it, we just wake up and repeat the same day we did before, not really understanding what our purpose is and what direction we're moving toward. More popularly known as "Same Sh--, Different Day." So if you've ever had the experience, or had the feeling or thought, *what am I doing here? What's life all about? What's my purpose? Am I really here just to get up each day to go to work, pay the bills, take care of the yard, go home, and repeat the process the next day and the day after and the day after?* If you're struggling with that question, this chapter is for you. I certainly had those thoughts.

A good starting point would be to develop new habits that will set you on your way of creating more success. Start a "To Do" list and prioritize it from most important to least important each and every day. This will begin to develop the habit of being a doer. When you start your day by tackling the most difficult task first, evidence is shown that this creates the habit of becoming a world-class achiever. Let's face it, if we handle the most challenging task of the day first, then we're going to feel like a champion— like there's nothing that can stop us and that we can accomplish anything. Imagine if you do this daily, weekly, and monthly, how that will expand your success consciousness. You'll quickly become someone who gets things done. In fact, this will increase your productivity so much you'll soon be running circles around those who only talk about getting things done.

This begins the process of becoming a Goal Slayer. At first start small; it will build the momentum of how you view yourself. When we begin to see ourselves as doers and achievers, we begin to reprogram our subconscious mind and, naturally, we begin to take more action and become more results-orientated. If you're noticing a theme here, then you've been paying attention. Everything starts by reprogramming the subconscious mind. All habits and behaviors are seated in the subconscious mind. When we change our mind, we change our destiny.

As I was mentioning before, 95% of our daily activities are habitually rooted in the subconscious. We get up the same time, use the bathroom, brush our teeth, take a shower, eat some breakfast, drive to work or school, and perform our daily routine. Then we get back in the car, drive home, prepare dinner, have dinner, clean up, watch some television, crash and repeat that same day over and over and over again. Things get so repetitive, often times many of us will arrive at work and not even remember how we got there. We're on autopilot; we sit in the same chair, we have the same conversations, listen to the same music, eat the same foods, and watch the same shows. Are you bored yet? Don't feel bad, a majority of people live like this their whole lives. Studies have shown that 95% of our habits originate from the subconscious mind. In other words, we go through our daily routines many times without giving any conscious thought to what we are doing. We become mind numb. We're on autopilot with thoughts and behaviors, as well as our physical activities. So, if we're going to change our life, we've got to begin to change our habits and change our thoughts.

There are very few tools like goal-setting that will begin to change our habits and reprogram those habits of success into our subconscious mind. The first thing is to identify what new habit or behavior we want to create. Then we must remain disciplined and consistent to allow the subconscious mind to rewire itself, building new circuits, thus making this new way of thinking the norm. At the same time, this will break the old negative programming. Some examples of these negative, self-limiting thoughts are, *I can't change, I'm not good enough, it'll never work for me, I'm not smart enough,* blah, blah, blah—the list of negative programming dialogue we have within our minds seems endless.

Consider that, on average, we have roughly 68,000 thoughts per day, and science has shown that nearly 80% of those thoughts are negative. We are regularly programming the subconscious mind with negative, disempowering thoughts. Goal-setting is the action of creating new habits and new empowering thoughts. The cool thing is anybody can learn new habits. It's simply the process of developing new skillsets and new thought patterns. If we want something different in our lives, then we need to take new action to get different results. Developing new skillsets and new thought patterns is no different than learning how to ride a bike or learning how to play an instrument. It takes practice, repetition, commitment, and discipline. The rewards are immeasurable. As I mentioned when I first started goal-setting, I never wrote them down. Therefore, most of my goals never became reality, and I became frustrated with the process. I found myself thinking that goal-setting was merely one of those "pie in the sky" concepts that wasn't grounded in any reality or truth. But once I learned the process I'm about to share with you, that all changed.

I encourage you to learn this process and implement it as soon as your path becomes clear to you. Once you have applied all the success habits discussed in this book, you'll find that your life begins to fall into place. You'll find a greater sense of clarity—more calmness and certainty than ever before. Your purpose will define itself, revealing a new path and setting you up for great success. Happiness and success is simply a process of changing your mind. Now that you have the tools to make that happen; your life will never be the same.

I encourage you to share the information in this book with everyone you know. We have a world in great need of healing. That healing can only occur with love, which is the dominate positive energy of the universe. When we share from our knowledge and our hearts, we are giving out of love.

Enjoy the journey; it's where the magic of self-discovery exists.

The seven steps to become a goal Slayer.

Step number one: Create Clarity

Decide what it is that you want and what it is that you desire to achieve in your life. It's really simple. Start by asking yourself, *what's important to me?* As I mentioned in the dreams chapter, we need to be thinking big thoughts, whatever it is that inspires us. To get our mind into the creative thought process, start by considering what's possible. Once you have an image of what it is that you want to create, the next step is to put it on paper.

Step number two: Write It Down

Someone said a long time ago, a goal that is unwritten is merely a wish. There is a kinesthetic process of writing your goals down that drives your goals deeper into your subconscious mind. Let me explain that a little further. The process of writing it, and putting it to paper, creates new nerve pathways and firing of the brain that syncs with the subconscious mind. This also is a critical step to rewiring our brains.

Step number three: Create a Timeline

Without a timeline, there becomes no sense of urgency. This will help us overcome inertia. So, for example, you decide that you want to improve your fitness; you want to lose 10 pounds and run a 10K. It's February and you want to accomplish this by June 1st. The timeline that you create will push you to take action to see your goal become a reality.

Step number four: Chunk it Down

Think of the things in your life you would like to change, and where do you need to start? For example, if you want to run a 10K and you haven't run up to this point, perhaps start with running to the end of the block a few times. It won't be long before you're running a mile, two miles, three miles and more. You can do the same thing with any goal you set. Chunking it down means making sure you keep it simple and attainable in the beginning.

Step number five: Categorize

I previously referenced a book my good friends, Drs. Dave Braun and Troy Amdahl, wrote, *Oola: Find Balance in An Unbalanced World*. One of my favorite takeaways from their book is how they easily define the seven key areas of life. They term it the 7 F's of life. They defined those as faith, family, fitness, field, finance, fun, and friends. These 7 F's define the categories within which we set our goals.

Step number six: No More Than Three

Research has shown that keeping the number of goals per category to three or less maximizes the likelihood of achieving them. Avoid falling prey to the laundry list trap. Those same studies indicate that a list of 10 or more within each category drops your chances of success to virtually zero.

Step number seven: Review Daily

I can't emphasize how important this step is in the process. Read your goals every morning. The more you review your goals, the more likely they will become your reality. I also recommend you put your goals in places like the opening screen of your smartphone, on your computer, on your mirrors, or in your vehicle; anywhere you have an opportunity, to review them frequently. The more you do, the more you read, the more you review, the more energy you create that taps into the infinite potential of the universe to attract and make these goals become real.

Step number eight: Get Started

There's no better time than now to write your goals down. Get over the fact that this is potentially hard. As I'm sure you've all heard, anything worth achieving takes hard work and sacrifice. If you really want it badly enough, you'll take action. The good news is the sense of achievement you'll have as you implement this process into your life will be like nothing you've previously experienced. You'll feel more committed; you'll have more direction and more clarity. I know of no other habit that successful people have in common than writing their goals down.

You can't begin your journey without knowing where you want to end up.

Eliminating the Obstacles to Goal-Setting

1. What previous thoughts or beliefs do you hold about goal-setting?

2. How would letting go of these old beliefs serve you in a more positive and productive manner?

3. What would your life look like if you set goals regularly and accomplished them?

4. What date do you plan on implementing goal-setting into your daily success habits?

CHAPTER TEN
"ABOUT THE AUTHOR"

*"Life isn't about finding yourself.
It's about creating yourself."*

~ GEORGE BERNARD SHAW

Jay LaGuardia DC, CCWP, has been a lifelong learner in the fields of physical fitness, nutrition, wellness, neurology, neuroscience, brain function, and the habits of success. After graduating from Ocean County College in New Jersey, he attended Life University in Marietta, Georgia, where he eventually received his doctorate of chiropractic. At that same time, Dr. LaGuardia married his college sweetheart, Dr. Pam, who eventually moved them to Eau Claire, Wisconsin, where they now reside. They have been married for over 27 years. Together they have three children: Alyse, Anthony, and Taylor—all of whom are successful in their chosen paths. Together, Dr. LaGuardia and his wife enjoy traveling, exercise, their dogs, and any new adventures in life that they can find.

Over the years, Dr. LaGuardia has been on the board of directors for many different organizations and businesses. These experiences eventually led to him becoming the President of the Chiropractic Society of Wisconsin.

His post graduate work included a special certification awarded by the International Chiropractic Association on wellness and lifestyle. His clinical experience found Dr. Jay working in, and eventually becoming an owner of, one of the largest and most influential chiropractic clinics in the world. In a career spanning over 25 years, he has been a mentor to many individuals on both business and personal development. Dr. Jay is a highly sought-after speaker, having lectured throughout the United States and internationally, as well to groups numbering in the thousands. His topics are wide-ranging, but often focus on maximizing human potential. His simple yet powerful teaching approach has been known to inspire his audiences.

APPENDIX: VALUES

Abundance
Accountability
Advancement
Adventure
Ambition
Appreciation
Authenticity
Balance
Being the Best
Benevolence
Brilliance
Calmness
Caring
Charity
Cheerfulness
Civility
Community
Commitment
Compassion
Confidence
Congruence
Collaboration
Contribution
Creativity
Credibility
Curiosity
Daring
Decisiveness
Determination
Dependability
Discipline
Driven
Empathy
Encouragement

Enthusiasm
Ethics
Excellence
Exercise
Fairness
Faith
Family
Fitness
Free Time
Friendship
Flexibility
Freedom
Fun
Goals
God
Generosity
Grace
Gratitude
Growth
Happiness
Health
Honesty
Humility
Humor
Independence
Individuality
Inspiration
Intimacy
Integrity
Intelligence
Intuition
Joy
Kindness
Knowledge

Leadership

Learning

Love

Loyalty

Meditation

Mindfulness

Motivation

Nature

Never Ending Personal
Improvement

Nurturing

Innate Potential

Optimism

Open-Mindedness

Organization

Originality

Passion

Peace

Perfection

Personal Development

Playfulness

Proactive

Professionalism

Punctuality

Quality

Recognition

Reliability

Resilience

Resourcefulness

Respect

Responsibility

Responsiveness

Risk Taking

Security

Selflessness

Self-Reliance

Serenity

Service

Simplicity

Social Responsibility

Spirituality

Stability

Success

Team Work

Thankfulness

Thoughtfulness

Trustworthiness

Traditionalism

Travel

Trustworthiness

Unconditional Love

Understanding

Uniqueness

Usefulness

Vision

Warmth

Wealth

Wellness

Well-Being

Wisdom

Work

THANK YOU
GIFT PROMOTION

Visit http://www.DrJayLaGuardia.com

Enter Name and Email Address

or

Email

Info@DrJayLaGuardia.com

Follow on Twitter @DrJsuccesscoach

Go to his web site

and receive a special gift subject to

availability.

Printed in Great Britain
by Amazon

22880732R00066